KU-379-079

Guinevere in Baltimore

Shelley Puhak

POETRY LIBRARY
SOUTHBANK CENTRE
ROYAL FESTIVAL HALL
LONDON SE1 8XX

WAYWISER

First published in 2013 by

THE WAYWISER PRESS

Bench House, 82 London Road, Chipping Norton, Oxon OX7 5FN, UK
P.O. Box 6205, Baltimore, MD 21206, USA
http://waywiser-press.com

Editor-in-Chief
Philip Hoy

Senior American Editor
Joseph Harrison

Associate Editors
Dora Malech Eric McHenry Clive Watkins Greg Williamson

Copyright © Shelley Puhak, 2013

The right of Shelley Puhak to be identified as the author of this work
has been asserted by her in accordance with the
Copyright, Designs and Patents Act of 1988.

All rights reserved

A CIP catalogue record for this book is available from the British Library

ISBN 978-1-904130-57-4

Printed and bound by
T.J. International Ltd., Padstow, Cornwall, PL28 8RW

Contents

Contents

Contents

Foreword

What always surprises foreign readers who happen to come across an anthology of American poetry is the variety of styles. While poets in older cultures know they are working within a tradition and de facto bear the weight of that tradition, what may be the most attractive and interesting characteristic of American poetry is that its practitioners have never been able to agree what it is, which has freed each poet to pretty much start from scratch, treating the past as of little use when confronting the present. Our best poets, beginning with Whitman and Dickinson, have little in common with one another and often give the impression that they come from some other country, one which, for reasons that are unclear, is also called the United States. If there's anything that unites our poets and distinguishes them from those in other countries, it is an obsession with private experience at the expense of experience they might share with others. In a huge country with a short history, more faith in religion than in culture, and no firm sense of its own identity as a nation, what our poets have left to lean on, for better or worse, are their own selves. In the last hundred years this has resulted in a lot of fine and original poetry, despite the always-present dangers of solipsism and narcissism that tend to accompany any disproportionate focus on the self.

It is refreshing, therefore, to come across a poet like Shelley Puhak, who shows more curiosity about the lives of other people than she does about her own. Dramatic monologue is her preferred mode. In her first book, *Stalin in Aruba*, there are poems written from the points of view of the women in the dictator's family, some of whom he later had arrested and shot; the unfaithful wife of the secret police chief who comes home too tired from torturing people to make love; and the five girlfriends of Hitler who committed suicide. Another group of poems is based on gravestone inscriptions, imagining the lives of the schoolmistress, the young wife dying in childbirth, and the parish priest who are buried under them. For Puhak, the ignored past continues to haunt us. In the wonderfully ironic and funny title poem of that first book, she pastes the face of Stalin onto an American photo of the famous vacation island in the Caribbean, using the technique the dictator himself was in the habit of employing. Puhak has a mischievous streak in her poems and delights in startling juxtapositions. Of course, when her subject is some dark chapter of history, the intent is not just to sweep the readers off their feet, but to remind them of an essential truth: that the banal and the horrific often coexist side by side, even in the midst of tragedy.

Her marvelous and far more accomplished new book returns to that theme, though in an entirely different setting. In place of real people one could read about in history books, we find ourselves in the world of legendary King Arthur and his court, except, as we quickly discover, this is a story of adultery among contemporary well-to-do Americans. What we have in *Guinevere in Baltimore* is a delightful blend of stock characters, and a style that combines the lofty manner of courtly romance with a tough vernacular mixing words and phrases from banking, medicine, biology, popular culture and fashion, to depict worldly ambitions and sex. King Arthur is a powerful CEO in high finance, neither wise nor very dignified. Guinevere is his unfaithful, bored wife, and the aging playboy Lancelot, who sits on the board of the same company, is her lover. They address one another in separate poems and explain themselves. The master of ceremonies for this thoroughly entertaining series of comic and erotic poems is someone called The Speaker, who, as in classic theater, addresses the audience and comments on the other characters. Puhak enjoys wearing masks in her poems, yet there can be no doubt that what are being described here are the lives of real people.

What makes *Guinevere in Baltimore* work as a whole is the sheer brilliance of the individual poems. The finest poetry, the kind one wants to keep re-reading, mostly comes down to memorable turns of phrase and vivid detail, and that is what one finds here. Of course, for a language to come alive for the reader one has to hear the voice of whoever is speaking in the poem, which requires verbal imagination and an exquisite ear for how different types of people talk. *Guinevere in Baltimore* is masterfully crafted, a veritable feast for any lover of words. Being a story about marital infidelity, its poems are full of things both intimate and scandalous. And juicy gossip, as the old Greek and Roman poets knew well, and made sure to record, will outlast empires and even gods.

– Charles Simic

Dramatis Personae

THE SPEAKER: neither Maid, Wife nor Widow, yet really all, and therefore experienced to defend all

GUINEVERE: the Queen

ARTHUR: her Husband, CEO of Camelot Transatlantic Shipping and King of the Britons

LANCELOT: her Devoted Lover; alternately, Arthur's friend and Most Trusted Salesperson

ELAINE OF CORBENIC: alternately, of Chicago; daughter of the Fisher King, Keeper of the Grail, Seducer of Lancelot, and Mother of GALAHAD, their issue

With Special Appearances by:

THE COURT PHYSICIAN and THE FINANCIAL MINISTER

THE COURT TROUBADOUR and LADIES-IN-WAITING

TWO GREAT CONFLAGRATIONS and ONE HURRICANE

Betsy Patterson Bonaparte, BELLE OF BALTIMORE,
and VARIOUS LOVERS

Presented as it has been played sundry times in quaint BALTIMORE TOWN, Jewel of the Chesapeake and Capital of the Land of Pleasant Living

And in the Summer I grew white with flame,
And bowed my head down: Autumn, and the sick
Sure knowledge things would never be the same

– William Morris, *The Defence of Guenevere*

*

On Having Sex, Grief-Stricken

Summer underfoot: toads,
vipers, adders and serpents,
even ambulances, and in
the eaves, chipmunks, and on
our napes, the rubber paw
of the attending.

Driving home, the car clings
to the yellow line and I will it
to cross over. You pull over
for gas, but can only beat
the car with the pump handle,
over and over, metal on metal.

And somehow – a hotel.
Easy-care earth-toned
bedding, claw-foot
in the corner. We can't
look at one another.
I straddle you, sobbing.
I'm stunned our bodies
can still screw
together, the threads
can catch: what has
steeled in you winding
up into my wooden.

An Infomercial for the Ladies-in-Waiting

When you find yourself on a fiscal cliff,
      overfull of participles – *going, going, gone* –
ashen, cashless, and tempted to trickle down;

      when you find yourself in an engagement
long-deferred, overdrawn even, with a stoop-
      shouldered duke with an ill-trimmed beard,

or his son, strumming Dylan on an ill-tuned
      harp, know this is a real medical condition
and the Troubadour is here to help.

      The Troubadour! Drop off your precipice
and convene an amorous congress. Sequester
      yourself with his kisses. Of course,

the Troubadour comes with some risk –
      decreased appetite and dry mouth. He'll get
your heart rate up, spending all the coins

in your twig basket, then asking you to cover
      his rent. The nerve! The tenor
on that one! He'll never stop, drowning out

      the memory of your mother's voice.
He'll sing through *Law & Order* reruns, immortalizing
      your soon-to-be sagging breasts –
                  going, going, gone –

Guinevere, Facing Forty in Baltimore, Writes to Lancelot

Turn it all off. Light a candle to read this
    and then unplug the toaster, unhitch
        the cable, the WiFi, break the heart

of every circuit, shut it all down.
    The king's satellites are circling,
        tracking our ambling hearts even here –

not upon stacked Belgian block but
    earlier, actual cobblestones. And
        the king's satellites are neither hungry

nor lonely. They won't scratch and scratch
    until they scab. But dear, how I itch
        electric. So I'm on my way, tripping

cobblestones, each ridged like a hipbone.
    I imagine them pitched at my head.
        Not the crack when they connect

but the wind when they miss. *Adulteress.*
    Love, his satellites are circling, his cell
        towers are triangulating. So don't call.

And burn this. Then blow the candle
    out and wait. Wear your armor.
        What's a little extra weight?

*

The Debt Ceiling

Outside D.C., under a dome of heat
and digression, I dream my usual:

houses. Chalets, mansions, usually
my college apartment. I return to a cat

I've been starving in the basement. Once
it was a giant tortoise. Another time a child,

misshapen, staring at me through the spokes
of its ribs. As if I owed something, and in this heat –

could the sky press any more? The day
is long and shapeless, and I wander

into the store, forgetting my intent.
Was it eggs? Was it bread? Back home,

on the television, men circle and seat
themselves at long tables. As if we could

meet our obligations and stare them down.
I abandon family to doze, slick under a sweat

ceiling, into a new house: quiet, orderly, empty.
I lead a long man of cooling stone up a long

staircase, to a landing with longer windows,
curtains half-drawn to the oddest light, late

afternoon or something quite like it. What
do I owe you and when are you coming for it?

Lancelot, En Route, Stopping Off at Fort McHenry

O say, can you see? – from 95 North, the swath
of city from stadium to incinerator smokestack

jutting up like teeth too-crowded in the bay's
small mouth. I've seen and Ginny, darling,

I can no longer breathe. Throbbing, I got off
the interstate, cut through an industrial park.

Then I saw an alley named Excalibur Drive.
How could I not pull over and sob?

My heart is, apparently, impure, clotted up
with more than cholesterol. In the afternoon meeting,

I was pulled off the Grail. The account went to one
less jaded – my own bastard. Damned Galahad,

kicked out of Oberlin, thrice, now sitting in Seattle rain
every weekend, protesting, waterproof in his Patagonia

and linked up with his iPhone. There's ignorance
and then there's innocence. If you don't want me, Ginny,

I don't know what will weigh me down. There's gravity
and then there's being grave. I rode the rim of highway

like the crease of your lips, searching by the twilight's
last gleaming. This fort offered succor. Here the sky

is spangled with spiral galaxies and the bay refracts
the dream of their strange light, a luminescence

gone liquid. Ginny, there's even light glinting
off your fillings. There's a city stuffed in your mouth.

Arthur, Pantoum for an Empty Table

We were two but it seemed there was a third
walking the white road home, the city wavering
before us. At the table bare, its varnish chipping,
we waited for servants who had already fled.

Walking the white road home, the city wavered
through fields of genetically modified grain. In the manor,
we sat waiting for servants who had already fled.
We ransacked the larder and then grazed

in fields of genetically modified grain. In the manner
of those face-lit clocks, we screwed with time.
I ransacked your larder and then I lazed
beside you, hooded. In the corridor, watching,

those faceless clocks. When we screwed last time
we were two but it seemed there was a third
beside you, hooded, or in the corridor, watching,
or before us, at the table bared, varnish stripped.

*

The Financial Minister Writes to Arthur

                              I share this with you
and only you, of course, although the Board
has thrice requested some report.

We spent three days thrashing through
larch and linden to find this village,
to scatter the lost fox-kits rimming its edges.

Your subjects are forthcoming
with ale and roast rabbit; overly-familiar
and quick to snatch up our oranges.

The Old Men refuse to give up
their mistresses, despite *we're in this together,*
et cetera, et cetera.

The Old Women twitter that the devil
is a child wearing a red cap and our Queen
has been kidnapped by wild beasts, a rival king.

What methods, what other means,
are at my disposal? I've stayed on message:
we're closing the loopholes. Building

a new mall. They must budget their love
more carefully. The Young brandish credit cards,
demanding to know what a King, any king,

might know of love's austerities.
The kits have circled back, mewing
so incessantly my attachés can't consult

or calculate. Three days hard travel,
then an entire fortnight unaccounted for.
Have we overspent our time? Please advise.

Arthur, Screwing with Lancelot in the Starbucks Line

– and frankly, Lance, between friends, I'm falling
apart, with this merger and the Board calling

for you to resign. The old observatory –
remember bringing flasks and girls up on weekends?
Can I ask if you recall –Stephanie? Tiffani? –

didn't everything end in an -ee back then?
Like Ginny, Jesus – poor, poor Ginny. When

she returned, she was already flush with fever.
Now, mornings, seventy sit-ups, then she piles
her hair up to pout in the bathroom mirror.

For hours. I'm amazed at the way light attaches
to a woman's nape, how her stray hairs can snatch

reason away – the overhaul of her underwear
drawer. Also the scabbing and scratching. How
her complexion is consumptive, how she stares

at the carpet, smiling at some spot or
stain. My satellites chirp. As do my doctors.

Lance, I fear our queen has picked up some
parasite. I'm afraid to ask what she
was doing – hitchhiking? – across our ocean.

The Manor Maids Petition Their Lord

Forbeare to charge women with Faults which
come from the Contagion of Masculine Serpents.

We tend table, keep knives
angled, napkins folded, just so.
You crack quail eggs, suck

marrow, slap table and hiss
of our sisters: Lewd,
Inconstant, Over-Fleshy.

In the scullery, we press poultice
and siphon this Venom,
becoming as underground ether,

lighter than Luchre but more
patina'd. Only our mistress'
chevel-glass reflects us back.

Recall that you were cast out
of a Garden. We grow one within.
We scrub up while its ivy twines

our cartilage. Listen to the rustle
of trees growing. The wind through
columbine and rue. Our Lord, quit

your Slither. Gentle Man, come back
to bed. Lie here and stretch
upward, kiss the Figs of our wrists.

*

Guinevere, Fancying Herself a Wanton Microbiologist

This honeybee.
        A fly lays an egg in its
abdomen (how? the literature isn't
      specific). Three nights later
that poor parasitized bee slips out
      of the hive, compelled to strange light.
Fly larvae spill out as the bee dies
      trying to nuzzle a porchlight.

This mouse.
        The protozoa lost in its
mouth (how? how should I know?)
      would rather live in the gut of a cat.
So it convinces the mouse to saunter
      right up to a cat. Snap.

Just as a parasite in the right
brain of the wrong woman (how?
      she's stuck cleaning the litter box!)
compels: leave the engine running,
      walk the razor's edge.

This girl –
       just a slip, a shadow,
     when she first stole
across the courtyard to meet you.
And so: I edged off the ledge of
      the castle walls. Compelled.

Lancelot, at the Home Depot

If I can stop the weeds, start the savings, can we still
be tender upon my fresh-mown fescue? So you

won't claim I'm triangulating things, won't complain
about the clot of mosquitoes in the unfinished pond,

the pearls of grubs under the back lawn, I'm
anticipating pests I never knew before: thrips the size

of iron filings, chinch bugs siphoning sap from
the grass, cherry-oat aphids crippled wingless

as they age – pests never sated, only staved off.
And for those that plague us nights inside, they've got

bedbug foggers, fire ant bait – all 30 % off!
This morning I found a groundhog chattering

in my new trap. He earned free shipping to the state park.
I still need some twine, stakes, a chainsaw for

the sick elm, wire snips for this space and time
continuum. Objects in motion, you see, experience time

slowly, too slowly. Truly – the hands on your
encrusted anniversary watch lag behind whenever you fly

home to Camelot. I'm outpacing you, darling, but I'm all
about more saving, more doing, whatever it takes.

And soon the salesman will return with just the right
pesticide underarm and *proof*: a brochure full of

photos of dead aphids, woolly with fungus,
their mouths still sucking the dew off the leaf.

Arthur to Guinevere, while Watching Occupy Wall Street Unfold on the Evening News

I've just read of those *Schistosoma* worms,
with marriages more stable than
the humans they inhabit. I've learned

> of this snail fever, this disease their loyalty
> breeds: eggs in our bladders, buoyancy

in our blood, cling and twist, pile and chafe.
Their mating clots us up, creates
an ache between our legs we might mistake

> for desire. My head to your breast, would I
> hear those worms sigh? There are pesticide-

laden apples, lead-coated combs. A dozen
things to fear. When the worms writhe, there's
no microphone small enough to listen.

> What to tell our subjects, what alibi
> for staying put when the weather's mild

and the sunset's pink with particulates?
Long-married, let's try to occupy
one another and forget the tents

> downtown, forget that you have fallen sick.
> Let's tell the court biographer the clouds were thick

with carbon, the doves snored, the horses dozed.
The pang between your legs was that of devotion.
Parasitic. And the briar arched up, enclosed

> all of us under its tent.

*

Searching for Baltimore

after Jack Gilbert

Not a fox. A rat. That nibbles my muffin-top, nudges
past my hips. That burrows between me and my

yellowed sheets and dreams the wharves too – Bond
Street, Henderson's, Broadway Pier – dreams the dumpster

scraps and the soft clutch of soil, dreams the dozen chambers
under each dock and the bay breeze that snakes through.

My rat. Tunneling the slink and sprawl of suburbs,
there were too many spaces between us but not

space enough to shunt love and haul it home. The train
since dismantled, we took to the automobile, my rat

and me, coupling and switching the tracks of our bodies
in the backseat. Arrived to find the city sealed up

against us, the trashcans empty at 3 a.m. And no subway,
but oh! – the sewers! My rat stayed but I slunk home,

scrabbled back up the roof and chewed through
the next three years. Made do with meadow until

they paved it over. Then hitched a ride back; got
an apartment; lined it with shredded paper, sacking,

cloth; looked up the rat and asked him out.
My rat, now grown both tall and fat, handles me

exactly as one spreads out the bedsheets, flapping me
out of myself, smoothing, smoothing – there, there, lay flat.

Guinevere, Supine

The claw, the fang, the webbed
    foot, the wet flapping – babies,
        supine and squalling, dream

same as our ancestors dreamt.
    Across the hall, electrodes know
        that the rat dreams the maze

most recent, the cat dreams the last
    stalking, while I dream the attics
        and streams of adolescence; I show up

at school naked; I lean in for the kiss and out
    tumble my teeth; I trace the maze
        of some strange house, stalked

by a copy machine. I'm back in
    Latin class, declining the supine,
        passing notes to you, full of

accusatives and ablatives.
    We break up between second period
        and the fourth declension. Here

I ought to write something
    wise. Here I ought to recline,
        supine as the full infinitive:

to sleep or to dream. Dear Reader,
    my tongue is in your maze. Keep
        your eyes closed while we're kissing.

Don't look – my whiskered
    twitch, my furred heave, my
        pale underbelly.

Lancelot, Prone

As for me, Reader, I tend toward old stone
houses – light misted up with motes

and every shelf and tabletop teeming
with deceptions, decorative and primitive.

Look, I'm liable to lie at dinner parties –
I'm really not the son of a senator

or the inventor of the post-it note;
I was raised by a fishwife I call Lady

of the Lake. And I'm apt to make it abstract.
For example: your tongue can twist

a few cherry stems into a mid-Atlantic
kingdom. And I'm the adverbial fly

in your ointment, face-down in your lap,
in the heroic pose of a B-25 bombardier.

I'm prone to rashes and overreactions.
I'm liable to send forth flares to silence

small lights below, my fire seeking
its own level, as water might. O Reader,

so far off, you flicker.
But you'll do.

*

Letter to an Old Flame

October, darling, you're impossible:

How early you get dark. And who will
          measure the gap between these
two animals, curled against your chill?

You wait for me in your woods at dusk.
          Up your street, a girl is borrowing fire,
leaning into an idling, unmarked truck.

Got a light? I've asked too, for a flint
          and firesteel to my fatwood, a cupped
hand so I might tend a spark in wind,

but you gave three men the Nobel Prize
          for proof that each day we lose more light,
proof we're to end not in flame, but ice.

The French still speak of *the little death*,
          but what of your small kindnesses, smaller
deaths? that chipmunk, maimed, I finished

off with a steel shovel? my backyard pyre
          of his old letters and your spent leaves?
What of that god who wants back his fire?

All I want: a warm brick for my bed,
          to be rid of the gap, that matchstick-
width that separates desire and dread,

to draw hard enough to keep it all lit.
          We always measure wrong. October,
what could you know of distance?

Your leaves, past flame, are carpeting
        cobblestones' muted blaze: scarlet, smoke,
and char. Layers. Who I was at fifteen,

how you still smolder. And his sweater,
        woolen, over button-down, starched, over
wisp of undershirt over –

        What we might make of the embers.

The Great Fire of Baltimore, 1904

The man who waters and houses
         me and my mother is so shrewd
    that by the time I stroll into school,
I'm already composing word problems –
                  winds
at 30 miles per hour across 70 city blocks,
and if 100 firefighters
            take the train down from Philly,
and their 76 hose couplings don't fit
    the hydrants, how much water
will icicle up the wires?
      When they let us out for lunch,
          I wind my way through
    bowing steel barons and off-kilter bricks,
the cursive of my footprints in the warm white
    ash of factory,
        phone company,
         post office,
          bank.
I'm searching for my father, my *real* father,
    the man whose morning cigar
             dropped
      into the grate
        into the basement
of the John Hurst and Company building,
    sparked stacks of Easter finery.
One painted wooden egg flared. Then, his smoke
        twined around my throat,
singing my cilia. My braids
    smoldering into ropes. I climbed them up
to the street, crawling out onto Hopkins Place,
          gasping down German Street,
staggering South Liberty –

POETRY LIBRARY

The Lexington Market Fire, 1949

Clutching handfuls of steel-
cut oatmeal to ash I wait, famished
in a single stall.

When the ice dealers open it
I gulp air and dash out,
overturning

tubs of daffodils, hyacinth, lilac,
tearing through aisles of victuals and viands,
my long hem dripping flames.

Lobsters death-whistle, boiling in their tanks
while pulled-taffy droops liquid, fresh-flaked
coconut snaps,

goose skin puckers, crisps, and off my lips I lick
its drippings. Outside, twenty-four engines, six
ambulances,

in the nearby hospital ready to evacuate:
new mothers ginger with fresh stitches and
leaking nipples

while I pop unshucked oysters, deep-fry fresh
muskrat, incinerate crabcakes and, with
their wax paper

melted in my teeth,
slurp up the juice at the bottom
of a smoking oak pickle barrel.

*

On Hurricane Agnes

I have friends upended by other disasters, bigger
trees down, swells the size of jungle animals, but
I am stuck on the hurricane that never left: Agnes
and her remnants, her Boones Farm breath

and Dunhill kisses – the disaster past, not
the one looming. We're already underwater,
as is our mortgage, and though we're strong
enough swimmers, it was not the waters

but what had seeped in that, back then, struck
all sick: sewage, solvents, and whatever leaks
from bodies, afloat and bloated. She's clever
like that. I was embryonic when she streaked

the sky violet, splayed bricks, tossed
car-husks. It's easy to romanticize her tantrum's
marker on the railroad bridge – Main Street
fourteen feet under. Until she swoops in

at the reunion, hurricane in hand, arches
an eyebrow and traces the creases
lacing my neck: *darling, you aren't looking so
hot.* I catch her in the coatroom, caressing

you through your best dress pants. I hold
my own hair, retching in the girls'
locker room, trying to figure out what she
managed, this time, to slip into the drink.

Guinevere Writes to Lancelot from
the Vacation Home in Sirmione

Lance, the light got more difficult,
      blazed russet, dripped liquid, once
            I broke those Jackie O sunglasses.

Squinting, on the verge of divorce,
      I stalked cobbles looking for dairy-free
            gelato and planning ways to win

the argument. All this before
      the storm forced Arthur and me
            inside. What light? Curtains of

rain pressed us up against the
      back wall of an open air restaurant.
            Water-logged, we tippled while

the *vigili del fuoco* put the world
      back together, unclogging the sewers
            so the streets could drain. How

stupid to think I was anything
      but vassal to and vessel for
            the rain. After all that money

for sunglasses! If water seeks its
      own level and God cares so little
            as to leave me pooled

at your feet, I'll head home, not
      ashes to ashes but down to
            the liquid in which we're conceived.

Betsy Patterson, after Meeting Jérôme Bonaparte, Dreams of a Pea, 1803

The storm whipped blue.
          Rain surged through the tips
of my slippers and back

out the heels, but still I came
          to city gates, latched like lips.
I had to insist I was real.

They probed my devotion,
          as if twenty mattresses, twenty
featherbeds could keep you

from mottling me purple. Now
          green. And I offered you plenty,
even my cheek. Come morning,

I climbed down, undressed
          for the ladies. Newly engraved
and electroplated – my spine.

They marveled: you had loosened
          the prongs, popped each vertebrae
and reset it, raw. Even my veins

were raised in revolt. So
          very sensitive, pathologically
sensitive, I must be worthy.

Some prince pulls me atop, rubs
          between my folds like sheets. Only
when he flips me back over,

what he mistakes for moans –
          my darling, my little knot of dopamine,
my constant dissatisfaction,

Betsy Patterson, after Meeting Jérôme Bonaparte,
Dreams of a Pea, 1803

my seed, my sweet Pea. You,
         a pearl of a jeweler, and me already
mounted. *Bind and bezel me.*

*

Guinevere, to Lancelot as He Watches
Casino Royale for the Third Time

My spaniels were bred to accompany me over
    glen, over dale, beyond the cold trail, past the clot
        of honeysuckle, through the neighbors' conversations,

their divorces and dumb waiters, to flush and retrieve
    something winged. Come to the river with us,
        see what we'll scare up. Shut that movie off.

I'm sick of its musical score's swells and the tide
    of your dick, sick of Vesper Lynd trapped
        on the freight elevator and you mouthing along

with Bond at the movie's end: *the bitch is dead.*
    You should see what I write about you
        in my secret notebook: you believe every maid

is wearing dagger-tipped stilettos, the heels
    venom-dipped. But I see too much, I say too much.
        Like this – these other dogs, wicked, one limping

something awful, that trapped a young deer
    midriver. She stood and took it, their tearing, done
        running and dying upright. My bitches couldn't kill

that way, bred to flush, bred for order. Small game
    only. And the movie is never true to the book –
        Bond never cradles Vesper's body on the Grand Canal.

He's never in Venice to begin with. But Bond does say
    the bitch is dead. Every good spy masters the art
        of the white lie: *I don't usually do this. I've never*

Guinevere to Lancelot as He Watches
Casino Royale for the Third Time

done this with anyone before. So I was bred to be your
  paramour in a glen, in a dale. Let's do it clandestine,
    while things winged wait in the bramble and thicket.

Arthur, on the History of Anxiety

which starts with the river and you who were lured
and we who languished, who took no
chances, said *I'm not going to try*

to float across on that and so survived.
Where the Patapsco is bridged with steel,
you launch that raft and someone else

paddles back through storm's
pooled light. One who wades
through daylight, reciting:

> *Hard rock of the piedmont begat tidewater*
> *plains, widgeon grass and wild rice. Begat*
> *mill and merchant prince, sailing vessel and*

> *steamer, begat things like sock garters and*
> *high silk hats. Begat what runs alongside:*

> *the snort of the steel horse and the huff*
> *of the mother, ever-steeled, who begat*
> *galloping heart and EKG machine.*

Oh, the authority of rivers and
the awful wall of us – *mast and sail,*

mortar and rust – pushing back.
And who is left to clean it all up? we

who took no chances, and so survived
to pick through your slough – cast-iron

skillet, rocking horse head, '67 Thunderbird
manifold, blue-glass chaff, electric typewriter

keys, garnet rosary beads, and the mill
workers' stone homes, brick by tumbled brick.

Guinevere, after Arthur's Appointment
with the Specialist

Arthur's prostate is enlarged. As is
    my liver. And my heart wants what the heart
        wants: a hamburger.

So after his biopsy at Hopkins, we went looking
    for a drive-thru that seemed safe enough.
        When we jounced over the old

streetcar tracks he winced. Eying up cornice
    and corbels on a boarded-up block he said, *Look
        what White Flight wreaks,*

but I misheard and thought he'd said *wife flight.*
    That's where my head is these days, ever since
        they stuffed me with sertraline

and asked me to breathe, deeply, the harbor's
    piss and old fish. No one extricated me when,
        across the street from that other Hopkins,

the university, I was jumped. Those children,
    and they were children, really, said *gimme
        what you got* and when I said, *I've not*

got either of them, they thought I was just trying
    to be funny. Lance, in our love the seed of all
        dismay that will follow. Arthur's

prostate should be the size of a walnut. The doctors
    continue to probe. Who would credit
        that a king should be counseled so?

*

The Court Physician Interviews Guinevere

What's the state of your conscience?

Here's one way to say it: we love
with the liver. No wonder I drink. And another:
we laugh with the spleen. No wonder
I find you funny.

Do you think you're being too flippant?

Does it matter what I think?
Guilt is not a dishrag, to be wrung out and reused.
It is always specific. It is always particular.

Does it matter what I think of you?

Only if you think a woman
more moist than a man. See, Lance leaks
everywhere. He sobs, he sweats.

*All the more reason to start manufacturing
distance.*

But I took the harbor tunnel here
without wondering if I was going to get stuck
while the bay started to seep in.

That's progress. What else?

Since I saw you last,
they invented and outlawed smoking.
So Lance and I tried swinging.

This seems sudden. And how did you find it?

Germ-ridden. And I didn't pick

the most flattering pants.

All the more reason to start manufacturing
distance.

But I've been busy laughing
with my spleen and speaking
with my gallbladder.

And loving, as you say, just with your liver?

Yes. Because it is many-lobed,
warm and humid.

Lancelot, the Microbiology of Us

Here's how I see it: there's a whole bachelor
camp pitching tents on the spongy turf

of your gut, illegals taking noon naps under
the shade of your cilia, department store

salesladies spritzing you fragrant and slinging
pearls of staph about your throat. Trillions

of microbes that weigh more than our brains.
Their three pounds outclasses the soul's measly

twenty-one grams. Here's how I see it:
last night both of us said some things

under their weight – I, the protozoa
that eats by engulfing; you, the amoeba

that slinks sidelong. But three pounds isn't too much
to carry. Guilt weighs far less. If our end feels like

the end of the world, that's because it is. Stay.
I'll love you through the fungus that will come

for us, first unearthed by bulldozers, now
cutting through air with tiny flagella tail,

coming first for the bee, the bat, the frog,
and then, obviously, you and me.

This fungus has already felled forests
of chestnuts, elms, pines, threading tentacles

into wood and slurping. It's airborne,
ready to shape-shift into a spore,

ready to wait out the slammed doors.

Guinevere, Dissecting Lancelot

Still wet from our dip in the river,
    you stripped off your shirt and so
        I found the freckle that straddles

your third vertebrae and from it traced
    the length of your spine. Then sawed
        through bone archways, stem to

sacrum, to get to the cord and its tortuous
    membranes. Tested my forceps against
        your most tubular bundle. Tugged

your palest tether. And carved out cross
    sections to sample your nerve.
        To think that I have the stomach

for this! – your slop in my stainless. Or the eyes.
    To read between your lines, reckon
        between vein and slimmest filament.

*

Lancelot, in the Apple Store

Excuse me, Knight of the Blue
Shirt and Untrimmed Beard, Knight of
Stylus and Screen, I'm seeking help
for my silvered one.

While you wait (it might be
a week or more), sample our newest apps. Do you need
to keep better tabs on her? Discern if she's menstruating?
Weigh her waist to hip ratio?

While I wait, I only need a quiet
spot to shed her zippered case, unhook her accessories,
recharge her fidelity.

That may prove difficult
with the older model. Have you sampled our newest,
fresh from the factory?

So thin, so pert!
I'm tempted, certainly. Fresh from the factory.
The factory. I see. Tell me, Sir, I heard
on the news there was a hand made into a claw
by your factory, a claw made into a hand
in your factory.

Don't concern yourself
with the clockwork of factories far, far away. Or the
temper of your own king. Her battery life will outlast
any love. Look – stroke her screen. Your finger –
press here, harder, here.

POETRY LIBRARY

59

Lady Elaine, Lancelot's Baby-Momma, in the Chapel Perilous

you pace the room enclosed
while I slip into something more
constricted   you slip into
me, another room enclosed,
while hyacinths wilt on
the nightstand   you slip into
me   (echo chamber for the exquisite
silence of ordinary people)
while my hippocampus
roars on   outside of us,
there is a freight train being loaded
by another man with gloved hands

you know what they say about
a man's hands   you know what I say:
Now, gentle knight,   (and we both know
you weren't gentle just then)   *kiss me but
once*   and yet you won't

our enclosure is rented hourly: ceiling
mirrored, TV chained   I finger
a hyacinth   you stalk
about in a towel, shrug
into a pressed shirt

gentle knight, (we both know
you weren't gentle just then) *whence
are you headed?*   I've already
boarded the freight train that barrels
through the dark night of the soul

I've already met the other man
with gloved hands   I know
what you will say: *to another chapel
to confess you*

Jonet Gothkirk to William Murdoch

This was the thirteenth day of Jonet Gothkirk's publick appearance in
Sackcloth for her Adultery… because of her Stupidity, and that she could
discover no sense or feeling for her sin, nor sorrow for ye same, she was
ordained to continue in ye place appointed for public Repentance –

I am Stupid in the same way
a treadle is duped into making
motion for the Machine,
Senseless as a shuttle, pass'd
betwixt and between Men
and their muscles, coil-sprung.

Oh, William of the last pew,
William of my roughest
wooing, what you weave
with those Fingers, nimble
and callus'd, threading through
one another, during my rebuke

from the pulpit, over, under –
my heart clatters! I know
Sorrow. That God so dour
crafted such a loom – those
Fingers, no smoother than
Sackcloth, but so fine, so long.

*

Confession for the Bromo Seltzer Tower

Truth is, I've always wanted you to shed that stone
    hard-on, slough off fifteen floors of mortar, brick
by brick, up to your steel ribs, until your

four-sided clock seems suspended, a star topped off
    with a falcon-filled aerie. A star of sodium
bromide, designed to tranquilize a hangover.

A star as sudden as the white of leg against the dark
    of car's backseat. Parked teenagers are distracted by your
wink: what sort of love is crowned with a fifty-one foot

bottle of antacid, over-blue, topped with its own tiara?
    Truth is, I'm cruel. I want all four of your faces trained
on me, tallying up the hours I dally downtown, watching

what I do with another under your light. Truth is,
    you're even crueler. You started how it all started: hiss
and fizz, bubbling up into stone. How do you stay stoic

when one of your falcons chases a wet pigeon
    into the clockworks chamber and your elevator motor
malfunctions again? Maybe it's easier with some girl

beached somewhere in Sandy Point, throbbing:
    If I was a Florentine fortress plopped down bayside,
if I was crenellated and someone climbed me.

Guinevere, Thirteen Reasons to Be Ardent about Euclidean Geometry

i.
Because in an airport café he sipped from a chalice
curved like a wrist while his steed's tail swished
through the suds of someone's beer.

ii.
Because he grasped
this drink as one grasps the wrist
of someone he plans to lead down a long hallway.

iii.
Because on the white plane of the love note
that summoned me there – since palmed damp –
exactly one line trailed off into the margins.

iv.
Because we were camouflaged by the fatigue
of the knights soon shipping out and blunted
by the ache of their families.

v.
Because there was a war
going on but he called it
a crusade.

vi.
Because in the airport café his shoulder blades
made a scalene and all our angles added up
to a flat line.

vii.
Because now, of course, he is in some other
city: we are a pair of coplanar lines,
everywhere equidistant.

Guinevere, Thirteen Reasons to Be Ardent
about Euclidean Geometry

viii.
Because there is
still
a war going on.

ix.
Because in the airport café
those knights were killing time, their ladies
talking too loudly for a Tuesday afternoon.

x.
Because given a plane
in space, there always exists a line
not on that plane.

xi.
Because I didn't want him
to get on
that plane.

xii.
Because when his steed stamped
and snorted, we finished
our drinks and left congruent.

xiii.
Because given space, I can name
the plane of his lower back –
glorious rhombus!

Lancelot, Fancying Himself a Playboy Astronomer

No friction in outer space – in such low density
a man might throw light great distances

without finding it refracted back by a former lover
on the water taxi or blocked by other celestial bodies.

Oh, all those strange terrains, molten cores!
Each singular in desire, ever-quirky in orbit. Say *parabola*.

Say *hyperbola*. Say I lack *escape velocity*. Say there's
an impending asteroid. Say I tell her so and

she unbuttons her blouse, thinking I've found
my way. But blindfolded, under overcast,

on windless, will I come back? A man steers
only by light and breeze. So I like to cup

a new tit, but always I loop back, orbit my first.
Trace her coordinates on the chart. While she circles me,

wet with beer and in want of weed. Once when I was
still young I woke to her on the ledge of my bed,

asking *Is there any more?* and in the dim
before I understood, we squinted.

*

Guinevere to Arthur, on Starting Over

Let's go back to Cornwall, back to
    the drawing board, back to being
        drawers, even, crafted to be drawn out

of some hulking antique. Let's hunker down
    into our dovetail joints – hand-hewn pins
        and tails same as neurons bundled,

same as language braided at the juncture
    of forest pathways: Old English *dragan,* to drag
        this out, and Old German *tragen,* to carry,

to bear your long silences. Let's slip off
    into a solid maple highboy. Let's squeak
        and get stuck. In each of us there's twilight

enough. There's one square of darkness
    framed out that each drawer is intended
        for. Let's wedge ourselves in and warp.

Lady Elaine, Lancelot's Baby-Momma:
How We Pose in Vacation Photos

i.
as hardscrabble, hands on hips,
as only stub and slit,
        in the parking lot of the factory
that ships out the notes and florals
                                of pheromones,
the one behind the strip mall, where we washed
        up off the highway.

ii.
as boiling foam and shoal
in eel grass, on tidewater coast
        rasping the world stern to bow
until its hull cracks in

                        the brackish thicket
upon beds of ponderous arks, knobbed
        whelks and moon snails.

iii.
as all heart, in a French café, kissing
for the camera, flashing
        our rings and pointing at our roasted
escargots. The moon is a wafer we've just
                                been offered,
but we're palming it until
        the next rest stop.

iv.
as all hunched, on the strand, sucking
lemonade through a straw
        while short-billed dowitchers pitch
and sweep the sky to sand.
                                Stage left,
you angle for bass, but only reel in three-
        spined stickleback.

Betsy Patterson Bonaparte to Her Brother-in-Law Napoleon, upon Landing at Dover Alone and Nine Months Pregnant, 1805

See, waiting for me to bear
or to burst, how they crowd – ?
My escorts must beat them back.
I can beat back what you fear
most – that all fires smolder out,
even the jaw so set will slack.

First moored in Amsterdam,
now stranded in England,
all your ports deny me entry.
Not as weathered, his hands,
as yours, I've heard. Let me land.
We'll talk. You'll bend. See

how I've bent what was brittle?
what I've softened and eased
round? Honed with my tongue?
What I know of you, what little,
you are too easily pleased
with gossamer, too easily stung.

Know it is not heat, but chill,
that governs my upswell
and that something climbs
into me at night too. Still,
I sweep a curtsy as well
as any courtier, easily find

my place. A merchant's
daughter, I know something
of exchange: I spend
only what I earn. Plant
to reap. Stitch and sing,
keep my ledger for one end.

*

Lady Elaine, Meeting Guinevere at the Employee Picnic

Your Majesty, even your side dish
brings his own side dish to the picnic.
We met at some mouth:
                    a tunnel, a river.
He was post-atomic; I was pre-hipster.
Lance looked like a man love-sorrowed
and book-sick, a man who needs
                    a drink, that's all.
I had a fancy chalice, and he was awed.
It was the waning of the oil age.
It was dopamine runs over the oil sheik
                        in the crosswalk
of the reward pathway. We piled
cigarette butts on the sidewalk
negotiating with Cornerboy for a little
                        enchantment, a chance
to outfox our constant selves.
We did our limbic thrust in the dark
of a downtown bower and he couldn't tell
                    the two of us apart.
What man can? He couldn't even
figure out the condom. It was all
wham! bam! baby! I was like
                    – *woah!*
you call *that* neurobiology's reward?
Still, I'll take *mother of* over *mirror of*
any old day. I'll take another deviled egg.

Guinevere, Meeting Lancelot at the Walters Art Gallery

Between mummies and saint's reliquaries, I hand you
   my liver in a canopic jar. You give me a gilded
      scrap of fingerbone in an NPR tote. We duck

under doorway slogans. *To virtue, add knowledge.*
   Ha! –we snort at that one. And then, as a redhead
      sways by: *Through such variety is nature beautiful.*

You gesture to an illuminated manuscript and say: *ink*
   clings. Meaning, of course, me. I wince under a wooden
      saint, holding his own head, dodge your eyes under

a marble madonna, baby god tugging her breast long,
   then pretend I'm intent on the butterflies of Maryland,
      the Baltimore Checkerspot and others, named for our

moods – Sleepy Orange, Northern Pearly-Eye, Clouded
   Sulphur – while you handle a learned astronomer's lens:
      Look at all I can draw close. Meaning, not me, but other

bodies, unbound by gravity. I demand my liver back, but you
   pin me against the glass, say it's time we left, say I'm being
      ridiculous. But the butterflies splayed beneath me

have long, tubular hearts and lack livers. They taste
   with their feet, hear with their wings, have no need
      for variety. The only color a butterfly sees: red.

Lancelot Questions the Clairvoyant

I've read sheep livers and intuited the yolk
of an unblemished egg. I've dusted off

my planchette and began again: *Spirits, what
should I do? Dress? Strip? Head west?*

Mystifying Oracle Ouija answers: *Yes. No. Yes.*
Did I tell you I signed the addendum? Shaved

my neck. Paid in full, three months early. Petitioned
the City Directors. Ginny said no more door-to-door

troubadours, no more serenades dedicated over
the airwaves. She said *go fuck Elaine*.

Madame Sosostris, what do you make of this?
I filled out the forms. I signed the addendum.

I sweated through the exam. I was told I was suited,
I was sought after. Madame, please stop

alchemizing antibiotics – that sinus infection, still? –
and soothsay. Tell me if dying is just rewinding back

to when I could carry my twelve-gauge
on the streetcar and no one blinked, back to when

mom and dad slept in separate beds, and under
the basement's single bulb,

Mystifying Oracle Ouija trembled
in her eggshell negligee: *Yes. Yes. Yes.*

*

Waiting Out an Election

because in times like these
to have you listen at all, it's necessary
to talk about trees.

Dear Reader, all's hollow and becoming smoke:
departed branches, my own ringed breath.

The logs are licchened, the chimineas are sparking
autumnal. I am full of mists and mellow

fruitlessness. So is it harder or easier to believe
that I am waiting to line up in a gymnasium

and tap multi-colored squares on a screen? or that
he left and I don't mind? I rather prefer the house

to myself, to rattle its plastered walls. All hollow. As
bird bones and feather shafts, as the mattress' sagging

valley, still warm, as an airplane's fuselage descending
into late summer's greenhouse of sweat and sadness.

As someone's leg, sloshing with drink. As that wooden
book you bought, trying to hide all your money from me.

As all those trunks propping up the canopy under which
he and I last kissed. Together, we might calculate

the hidden costs of pleasure – the pesticides, the
permits. Dear Reader, let's talk about trees, how

heavily veined, how susceptible. Beyond bark
and sapwood, inside heartwood – dark-colored,

dead. Or we might talk about rivers – coursing
behind the smoke, within the mirrors – talk about

the currents that cast hollow logs upon strange
shores. Dear Reader, I am willing but dry as kindling,

combustible as a ballot box. Oh, how pleasant
to forget that not love, but fear roots us.

POETRY LIBRARY

Guinevere to Lancelot in Role-Play: H.D. and Pound

In want of warmth after we had lain
                              on the hoar-frosted moss,
your arms braided the lowest
                              branches, your legs wrapped the trunk.
        You thought you *were* a tree.
You stood still and thought that was listening.

*

Does it matter what sort of tree
you thought you were?

In my grandmother's village
the oak is most powerful

        in my other grandmother's village,
        the linden tree

but during both of their weddings,
while the groom mimed knocking,

        someone shrieked
        from the altar:

Who goes there?
Are you fungus or friend?

*

Grass snakes in another

        village are allowed to live under the stove
        and lap milk from the cat's bowl.

No wonder the cat wanted out. To die in the wood, not

on the carpet where we kept setting her.
                              The grandmothers want in.
          They stroke bark and sniff leaf-gloss.
                              The trees tell them
it's time to go inside, take to bed,
lie down, lie still.

*

I'm stirring, spreading through your roots,
          up through your soles, your callused toes,
                    up through your hands too smooth,
                              through your leaves, thin and lacey –

Who goes there? Are you an enemy of trees?
Are you flood or fire? Insect or fool?

*

Your arms braided the lowest
                    branches, your legs wrapped the trunk.
          You thought you *were* a tree.

I could break a tree.
                    I can.

Lancelot, after Being Caught Downloading Porn

Look. When the arborist called – the old oak
in the yard was too far along –

I sobbed in the Target parking lot, recalling
the birch of your body and the oak

of my own desire, pyramidal in youth,
thinning in autumn. And the day after

the machinery came, the cat
had to be put down. O! the simplicity

of a needle after so many tools with teeth:
saws, chippers, grinders. I'd think the cat

imperative and the oak incidental
to our story, had the arborist not said

deciduous over and over, explaining how
this oak, startled as a sapling, had always

been hollow. And now even its stump
gone. Easy, too easy, to let the cat

crumple. Someone came with the needle, someone
hummed among the last fingers of leaf.

Look. A hollow tree stands only on the new
wood it urges up. I'm only hunting

for a bit of bark to peel back, the surprise
of the pale just beneath, the dappled

birch of any body. Put away your quivering lip,
my dear. We were always deciduous.

*

The Court Troubadour's Song for the Old Streetcar Track

I know all of your crevices, and each is
　　　　dreadful, my dear – sidewalk crack, mortar
joint, neuron gap. You must have invented

the ellipsis where crosstie and rail meet
　　　　but sold the patent for one pint more or
some magic beans. Whatever we have meant –

you and me – before asphalt and machinery
　　　　intervened, the stars are still cross with us.
You trail off into whiskey and sleeping wood

but I am grateful for small consistencies:
　　　　how all trees harbor some fungus,
how shadows leap, smoke winds, and I become

lulled by momentum – the rattle, the pant, –
　　　　that makes it seem we will go on whether
the trolley wire follows or not, seeking a new

point where your rails will never meet. I can't
　　　　slip into your spaces; you will never
fill my dark fissures. I am crossed with you.

Lancelot, Advising Galahad at the Office Depot

So you've fathomed an unfamiliar
flank. All the early bees of spring
swarm in your stomach and you're lax
and lucid with endorphins. Still,
be polite. Despite this recent upswing
in your prospects, don't forget the facts
of your situation. Send a note.
Handwritten, in a gilded envelope.

Merry wench, distressed damsel, enchantress
with a hard luck story: each one wants words,
wants some small song to wet the flap –
the smallest song, most lonesome, the longest –
wants a sonnet in an envelope creasing towards
closure, even if no glue will ever seal the gap.

Guinevere, to All of Her Unborns

The river's tent is not broken, but bent
                         enough to leave you exposed,
          my sweets, clustered on the shore of my pulse,
the wet clutch of my muscle.

Why I can't bring you indoors:
                         I carry the gene that makes
          one susceptible to rain. There isn't enough
oxytocin to go round.

The dolorous stroke is wrenching out
                         a rib to make another.
          And the wound that won't heal: women.
The story they keep telling:

that I am waiting to be sought.
                         That my men wander
          but I am lost in the cemetery where I went
one violet hour to sneak a cigarette

and startled a deer. A doe who darted
                         into traffic. Her fawn
          followed suit. River and current: one drags
the other along. Just as this land was never

my land: not my dust clouds rolling.
                         I hardly know my own mother
          tongue. They say the moon borrows its brilliance,
offers no light of its own. They say my river

runs soft, runs softly. Keep clinging to its bank,
                         my sweets. When I make my own map
          of the world, I'll sketch this shore, your pebbled
forms, in ochre and animal blood.

*

Snow White and the Seven Satellites

A star needs a satellite like a fish needs
a bicycle. Imagine seven bicycles. Imagine
so many spoked mouths gaping in the garage,

so many chains rusted so many
shades of almost-orange, of not-quite-brown.
Say it: yellow. Then imagine

my dwarves again – demoted Pluto and
his minions, bobbing in the cool
slake of the dark ocean of space.

*

Everybody wants a piece of me. Mr. Disney
insists on my heart in a box. The Brothers Grimm

want my lungs and liver boiled in salt. The Italians
want my intestines. The Spanish

want my blood in a bottle stoppered
with one severed toe. And Pushkin,

he binds me – to a tree. For the wolves.
For seven knights, mustached and ruddy.

*

Back to the seven bicycles, rusting.
        My astronomers never bother to look
        in the garage. And if they did! –
in all that rust, iron. And
in iron, shards of space rocks,
        from errant dwarves involved
        in stellar smash-ups. And

in every story, bits of pyrite –
  left to oxidize –
  fool's gold, iron sulfite.

The Last Meeting, along the Path to Arthur's Grave

Here – grass matted means
                              a deer path, white tufts in underbrush
        mean a doe dozed last night, her ears like satellites,
swiveling. Like any prey. Like us,
                              soon off to a hermitage, a convent.

Cowardly or clear-sighted, we'll hedge our bets
                              in hairshirts, woolen robes, woolen
        underpants. We'll sail silent corridors, praying
for early November snow –
                              remnants of stars wrung soft,

dawn's white lint. A prioress
                              will show us how God lives
        in the lens: a neuron is webbed same as a nebula,
same as a snowflake. How the cuckold
                              forgets the same as the cunt.

How we are never more alone
                              than in love. We'll illuminate manuscripts
        with sketches of spiral galaxies – discs
of light, bulging, luminescent breasts.
                              Darling, darling, who will forgive

that once we expected to suckle?
                              Here – his headstone. Under stars beating
        dawn back. Among these vegetative beds, no,
beds of vegetation. Next to a doe's skull,
                              her eye socket cracked.

Lancelot, Facing Fifty in Philadelphia, Writes to Guinevere

My raven, you scold: *swoosh, sweep, rat a tat tat,*
you must need a statin for that. Darling,

harbinger, know I hold you, fluttering,
within my rib cage. But don't write back.

Make a facsimile of me, folded and rolled,
attached to a pigeon's leg or memory's

wing. Photocopy me flat and mail me
to the editors. Remember me in good ol'

two-dimensional, not as a vast absence,
like my atoms foreign-born from a star

dying in the belly of a galaxy far, far
away; my empty atoms, 99 percent

blank space. Don't recall how we fly
at 220 kilometers per second through

our individual galaxies. Like you,
I mean to go off the grid entirely. Why?

I see just one percent of the spectrum,
whether electromagnetic or otherwise,

and I'm tired, Ginny, oh so very tired,
and even here in Clark Park, I see plums

piled in the trough of a housemaid's apron,
pesticide-free plums bursting into flame

in colors not yet charted, but always the same
shade as the underside of your tongue.

* * *

Notes and Attributions

Dramatis Personae

"neither Maid, Wife nor Widow" was the seventeenth-century equivalent of (humorously) calling someone a whore. Versions appear in Shakespeare's *Measure for Measure* and other works. This phrase in its entirety is borrowed from Ester Sowernam's 1617 *An Answer to a Lewd Pamphlet, Entitled The Arraignment of Women.*

"Lancelot, En Route, Stopping Off at Fort McHenry"

Francis Scott Key wrote "The Star-Spangled Banner" during the 1814 British bombardment of Baltimore's Fort McHenry.

"The Manor Maids Petition Their Lord"

The epigraph is from Ester Sowernam's *The Arraignment of Women.*

"Searching for Baltimore"

Jack Gilbert's poem, "Searching for Pittsburgh," begins: "The fox pushes softly, blindly through me at night/"

"Guinevere Writes to Lancelot from the Summer Home in Sirmione"

vigili del fuoco – Italian fire and rescue services (literally, *firewatchers*).

"Betsy Patterson, after Meeting Jérôme Bonaparte, Dreams of a Pea, 1803"

Betsy, the beautiful daughter of a wealthy Baltimore merchant, married Napoleon's younger brother Jérôme after a whirlwind romance. Shortly after, Napoleon ordered his brother back to France and had the marriage annulled so he could marry Jérôme off to a German princess.

"Guinevere, to Lancelot as He Watches *Casino Royale* for the Third Time"

Casino Royale is Ian Fleming's first James Bond novel; there is also a 2006 film adaptation. Bond's lover Vesper Lynd is a double agent who betrays him and then commits suicide because of her guilt.

"Lady Elaine, Lancelot's Baby-Momma, in the Chapel Perilous"

In Arthurian legend, the Chapel Perilous is the setting for a sorceress's unsuccessful seduction of Lancelot.

"Jonet Gothkirk to William Murdoch"

The epigraph is from the West Calder kirk session minutes, 25 November 1677, recorded on a placard underneath a sackcloth gown in the National Museum of Scotland.

"Confession for the Bromo Seltzer Tower"

This historic Baltimore structure was built by the inventor of the Bromo Seltzer headache remedy and modeled on the Palazzo Vecchio in Florence. It was originally topped by an illuminated replica of the blue Bromo Seltzer bottle.

"Waiting Out an Election"

The epigraph is from Adrienne Rich's poem "What Kind of Times Are These?

Guinevere to Lancelot in Role-Play: H.D. and Pound

Pound loved to compare his speakers to trees ("I stood still and was a tree amid the wood") and he used to call H.D. his dryad. H.D's. response in her poem "Garden": "If I could stir/ I could break a tree – / I could break you."

"LANCELOT, CAUGHT DOWNLOADING PORN"

The phrase "the last fingers of leaf" is taken from T.S. Eliot's *The Waste Land.*

"LANCELOT QUESTIONS THE CLAIRVOYANT"

The Ouija board was first marketed in Baltimore in the early 1890s. Madame Sosostris is the tarot reader in *The Waste Land.*

"GUINEVERE, TO ALL OF HER UNBORNS"

The phrases "the river's tent" and "runs soft, runs softly" are also taken from *The Waste Land.*

Acknowledgments

I am grateful for the editorial insight of Charles Simic and for the encouragement of my earliest readers, Carrie Addington and John Surowiecki. Many thanks to the editors of the journals in which the following poems first appeared, sometimes in earlier versions:

Barn Owl Review: "Lady Elaine, Lancelot's Baby-Momma, How We'll Pose in Vacation Photos"

Carolina Quarterly: "Guinevere, Facing Forty in Baltimore, Writes to Lancelot"; "The Court Physician Interviews Guinevere"; "Guinevere, after Arthur's Appointment with the Specialist"

District: "The Court Troubadour's Song for the Old Streetcar Track"

Fairy Tale Review (Yellow Issue): "Snow White and the Seven Satellites"

FIELD: "The Last Meeting, along the Path to Arthur's Grave"

Gargoyle: "An Infomercial for the Ladies in Waiting"; "Guinevere, Supine"

Jabberwock Review: "Guinevere, Meeting Lancelot at the Walters Art Gallery"; "Guinevere, Fancying Herself a Wanton Microbiologist"; "Lancelot, Fancying Himself a Playboy Astronomer"; "Arthur, Watching Occupy Wall Street Unfold"

jmww: "Betsy Patterson Bonaparte to Her Brother-in-Law"

Kenyon Review Online: "Lady Elaine Meets Guinevere at the Employee Picnic"; "Lancelot Questions the Clairvoyant"

Missouri Review: "Letter to an Old Flame"

Ninth Letter: "Guinevere Writes to Lancelot from the Summer Home in Sirmione"; "Lancelot, at the Home Depot"

The Normal School: "Lancelot, Stopping Off at Fort McHenry"; "Guinevere, Dissecting Lancelot"

The Pinch: "On Having Sex, Grief-Stricken"

Superstition Review: "Searching for Baltimore"

storySouth: "The Lexington Market Fire, 1949"

The Urbanite: "The Debt Ceiling"

Women Studies Quarterly: "Guinevere, Thirteen Reasons to Be Ardent About Euclidean Geometry"

Yalosbusha Review: "Betsy Patterson, after Meeting Jérôme Bonaparte, Dreams of a Pea, 1803"

"Waiting Out an Election" appeared in *Adrienne Rich: A Tribute Anthology,* Ed. Katharyn Howd Machan.

A Note About the Author

Shelley Puhak was born in Washington, D.C. in 1975 and grew up in Maryland. She holds an MFA from the University of New Orleans and an MA from the University of Delaware. Her first collection, *Stalin in Aruba* (Black Lawrence/Dzanc), was awarded the Towson Prize for Literature. Her poems have appeared in many journals, including *Carolina Quarterly*, *FIELD*, and *Ninth Letter*. She teaches at Notre Dame of Maryland University, where she is Eichner Professor of Creative Writing.

A Note About the Anthony Hecht Poetry Prize

The Anthony Hecht Poetry Prize was inaugurated in 2005 and is awarded on an annual basis to the best first or second collection of poems submitted. For further information, please visit Waywiser's website at

http://waywiser-press.com/hechtprize.html

FIRST ANNUAL HECHT PRIZE
Judge: J. D. McClatchy
Winner: Morrie Creech, *Field Knowledge*

SECOND ANNUAL HECHT PRIZE
Judge: Mary Jo Salter
Winner: Erica Dawson, *Big-Eyed Afraid*

THIRD ANNUAL HECHT PRIZE
Judge: Richard Wilbur
Winner: Rose Kelleher, *Bundle o' Tinder*

FOURTH ANNUAL HECHT PRIZE
Judge: Alan Shapiro
Winner: Carrie Jerrell, *After the Revival*

FIFTH ANNUAL HECHT PRIZE
Judge: Rosanna Warren
Winner: Matthew Ladd, *The Book of Emblems*

SIXTH ANNUAL HECHT PRIZE
Judge: James Fenton
Winner: Mark Kraushaar, *The Uncertainty Principle*

SEVENTH ANNUAL HECHT PRIZE
Judge: Mark Strand
Winner: Chris Andrews, *Lime Green Chair*

EIGHTH ANNUAL HECHT PRIZE
Judge: Charles Simic
Winner: Shelley Puhak, *Guinevere in Baltimore*

Other Books from Waywiser

Other Books from Waywiser

Greg Williamson, *A Most Marvelous Piece of Luck*

FICTION
Gregory Heath, *The Entire Animal*
Mary Elizabeth Pope, *Divining Venus*
Gabriel Roth, *The Unknowns**
Matthew Yorke, *Chancing It*

ILLUSTRATED
Nicholas Garland, *I wish ...*
Eric McHenry and Nicholas Garland, *Mommy Daddy Evan Sage*

NON-FICTION
Neil Berry, *Articles of Faith: The Story of British Intellectual Journalism*
Mark Ford, *A Driftwood Altar: Essays and Reviews*
Richard Wollheim, *Germs: A Memoir of Childhood*

*Co-published with Picador